Contents

Disclaimer

The words in this book are my opinion and based on my experience and are NOT medical advice. If you are taking medications such as anti-depressants or anti-anxiety, do what you will at your own discretion.

Anxiety Almost Ruined Me

It was January of 2012, around 8 in the morning and I was at church. The weather was cold and brisk in the southern state of South Carolina. At the time, my mom worked in the infant nursery and I used too, however this day, I decided to go sit in the sanctuary awaiting the first service to start. I do not recall anything being heavily weighed on my mind, however I started to feel a little weird.

Due to the winter weather, the heat was on in the building, but not to the level I started to feel. I felt as if I could not breathe, so I decided to walk outside to get fresh air. I remember being outside and that feeling of suffocation worsening with each step that I took towards my moms' car. Once I made it to the car, I called my mom, but she did not answer, so I texted my friend who also worked in the nursery to inform my mom that I felt like I couldn't breathe. Not long after, my mom and my siblings and I were on our way to the nearest emergency room.

I recall the drive there was one of confusion because I started to calm down in the sense of feeling like I could breathe normally again, just not one hundred percent. We got to the ER and checked in and I was put into a room with my mom. Different tests were drawn to make sure my vitals were in the clear. The doctor came back and said my tests looked normal and that I had a panic attack and anxiety. I was not okay with that diagnosis because I did not believe I was stressed or worried about anything, consciously.

That day turned into almost a year and a half of struggle. The previous year, I had failed at college and apparently it affected me subconsciously. All my life, since age 6 or 7, I always said I would be a Pediatrician and eventually own my practice. So, when I graduated high school in 2010 and started college in January of 2011, I was excited and ready to get this degree knocked out. However, due to financial reasons, by the end of that Spring semester, I was denied enrollment for Fall due to an $800 past due tuition fee. On top of that, the main classes I needed, I had to drop because I did not have the funds to buy the books for those courses.

Here I am, someone confident and sure of her career path eating her words that she has spoken for the past 12-13 years. If I am transparent, my ego and pride was bruised. My peers were thriving in college and they graduated with their bachelor's before I did. I began to hate college, the way they did things as far as curriculum because the classes I had to take, were the same ones from senior year high school. I was under the impression that I would only be taking classes directly related to becoming a Pediatrician. Clearly, I was wrong and misled.

So, it is now Summer, and I am back in my hometown having to return to the nursery to work, in which they no longer had room for me. I then applied at Walgreens and was hired July 2011. This was my first real job and it lasted for 6 months, when I decided to quit because retail was not and still is not for me. I started to feel stuck and less than, a lame. I was supposed to be in school. I applied for one of the hospitals through their PRN system to where they send you to work at different medical offices. I was hired the end of December 2011, but orientation was the last week of January 2012.

The anxiety/panic attack occurred the first week of January and I was super concerned since I had orientation coming up in a few weeks. I needed to work, but the way I felt, I was scared I would lose the job before my first day. Fast forward, orientation came, and I remember being in the conference room of the main hospital and they had carpet and the doors were shut, with lots of other new hires. That is significant because carpet made me feel stuffy, doors being shut made me feel trapped, and large crowds made me want to run away. Then it happened. I had to hurry and escape to the restroom because I started feeling like I could not breathe again. I was having a panic attack. I ended up leaving, but thankfully, I was able to re-attend the new hire orientation another day.

From February to August of that year, 2012, I experienced moments where I had to leave work early, lay down in one of the patient rooms, could not ride in the car with others, could not get stuck in any kind of traffic, could not attend church anymore, could not go anywhere without a bottle of water, could not dine at restaurants and could not be in the car without the windows rolled down. As you can see, anxiety and panic attacks were ruining my life. My family was not supportive. I felt like a black sheep in a way because they felt I was being extra or crazy. I would go on nature walks or sit by the river and just breathe and talk to God. I was depressed. I gained weight.

September 2012, I was talking to my dad, who was stationed in Texas and he offered for me to come live with him. I think I thought about it for two days and then the next week, on the ninth, I was driving 21 hours in my 2000 Nissan Sentra packed up and leaving South Carolina behind. I have been in San Antonio, Texas since September 10th, 2012 and that was the best decision I could have ever made. Not to say the panic attacks and anxiety suddenly stopped, but this is where I geared up for war and decided to take back my life.

What Is Anxiety & Panic Attacks?

The Oxford Languages define anxiety as being "a feeling of worry, nervousness, or unease, typically about an imminent event or something with an uncertain outcome." The American Psychological Association defines anxiety as being "an emotion characterized by feelings of tension, worried thoughts, and physical changes like increased blood pressure, sweating, trembling, dizziness, or a rapid heartbeat." Any of this sounds familiar? For me, I experienced the dizziness, sweating, and trembling.

Panic attacks are similar except they cause the intense fear and come suddenly. Its symptoms often feel like shortness of breath, nausea, or a racing heartbeat. The dizziness from the anxiety resulted in the fear of passing out which resulted in the panic attack symptom of shortness of breath.

I remember finding an article written by a guy who looked at anxiety and panic attacks from the black and white, scientific, straight to the point view. He said anxiety is simply your body naturally responding to fight or flight. That article is what shifted my mindset to be able to fight for my peace of mind. He said that in panic attacks, your body is telling you to fight or run away, however, you must go against what you normally do when you experience attacks. For me, running away, isolating was becoming my norm, so I started to sit still. I started listening intentionally to my breaths to control them. This was a daily fight for me.

You cannot do the same things and expect a different result. Sooner or later, you must decide to fight back and refuse to tolerate anxiety in your life. The thief (in this case: anxiety) comes to steal, kill, and destroy. Anxiety will do just that. It robs you of your peace, it limits what you can do, it limits your life experiences that are meant to be enjoyed. Had I allowed anxiety to rule me, I would have been stuck in the house. A scary thought.

False Evidence Appearing Real

We all have heard the saying that fear is just false evidence appearing real and for the most part, if not all parts, that is true. Let's think about it. When you experience(d) anxiety and panic attacks, *{for the sake of the rest of this book, we are going to call both anxiety}*, you were not doing anything fearful. You probably were minding your business, doing something innocent as watching television or eating a meal, or as I was doing, sitting in church waiting for service to start. There was nothing to cause us to go into fight or flight mode, so we can agree that our body was reacting off false evidence of danger.

The dictionary defines fear as "the unpleasant emotion caused by the belief that someone or something is dangerous, likely to cause pain, or a threat." The mind is our powerhouse. It is apart of our soul which houses the mind, will, and emotions. The ability to imagine and dream and create stories in our head is fantastic, but we must learn to control what we allow to roam in our heads. Our thoughts determine our life. What are you thinking on constantly? Are you thinking fearful thoughts or are you thinking about hopeful things? What do you believe is true?

Fear is only good to a point. Not wanting to feel pain because of a dangerous action is normal. Fear protects us in that instance. However, I believe fear limits us more than it protects us. Meaning while it preserves us, that preservation makes up only less than half of what fear truly does to humans. How many people are not doing what they desire to do because they're "scared"? Many. However, God says do not fear, so if God says not to fear, fear cannot protect us; it must be wisdom that protects us, and wisdom only comes from God.

Fear is rooted in the lack of love. It is also rooted in always wanting to be in control. The master fear is the fear of death. If we believed in our hearts that we are loved by God, we would not fear because perfect love casts out fear (1 John 4:18). Fear and love cannot exist together. I still struggle with fear on some type of level in the sense of I must feel I am in control. Keyword being feel because no one is truly in control of their life and what happens, supposedly.

Practical Solutions

The natural solutions mentioned were to do things like yoga and meditate and just focus on your breathing. I have always been a homeopath, if that is the right term, but basically someone who looks for the natural remedy versus the medicinal or western medicinal remedy. I did not want to be labeled. I recall establishing preventative medical care in Texas and the history questionnaire you complete always mention if you ever had anxiety and I would always lie and say no. I did not want anything regarding my mental health on file. It's a deeper story than that, but if you know me personally, I will share with you why I feel that way.

We all have one body, and we must fight to take care of it. We must be intentional about our health and remaining in excellent condition. Exercise and eating better, less processed, fresher, are great places to start. A lot of what is in our food, directly impacts our body natural responses and chemical makeup. The top 10 foods and drinks that can contribute to anxiety as told by U.S News are: desserts, sodas and other sugary drinks, processed meats, cheese, and ready-made meals, coffee, tea, and energy drinks, alcohol, gluten, fake sweeteners, and foods with high glycemic indexes.

For me, I applied what the guy in the article mentioned such as meditation, as well as standing on my Faith. I opened my Bible and searched out scriptures relating to peace, safety, love, not fearing, and healing. I remember going to the store and buying index cards. On those index cards, I wrote down the scriptures that built up Faith and Peace in me. Scriptures that made me feel powerful and that encouraged me. I carried that deck of cards with me every single place I went and when I felt a hint of uneasiness, I started reading the scriptures aloud. I did this daily until I memorized it and until I no longer felt attacked.

So, for you, you may want to start with meditation, cutting out bad food and drinks, exercising, and if you're a believer as I am, stand on scripture and be in prayer always.

Nine Years Later

I felt confident enough to say I overcame anxiety sometime in the latter end of 2013. I was able to start dining out again and being a passenger in vehicles. I will admit that I did not stop carrying water with me everywhere I went, but hey, that is not a bad thing; we need water. However, I will say, that I did not and do not freak out anymore when I realize(d) I did/do not have water with me.

It is now 2021, and life is so much better. I thank God truly for His word because His word is what kept me and keeps me with a peace of mind. Anxiety will always try to try you at random moments throughout life, however, once you learn how to fight and take control, you will be able to nip it in the bud at onset before it can become an issue. Nowadays, when anxiety attempts to rear its ugly, bald head (no offense to those who are bald, y'all are fine), I start taking authority over my body and mind. The authority Jesus has given me, through Him, I can boldly stand my ground and rebuke anxiety at its root, rebuke the symptoms, and start declaring what God says I am and what He says He has done and what He says I can have.

Rewinding back to when I said the master fear is the fear of death, well I think I am fifty-fifty over that. I still do not like flying, but it's not a crippling fear to where I will not do it if I must. Now, if I do not have to fly, I am not doing that honey. Where are my keys? So, there have been times where I felt weird {an unexplainable feeling} when I would take my late grandmother's stethoscope and fall asleep listening to my heartbeat. Or one time I had a scary experience at six flags fiesta, and it resulted in me buying a pulse oximeter which checks your oxygen level and heart rate, so I would check my vitals and when I realize all is well, I simply stand on my scriptures and be at peace.

I am learning that there will always be challenges as you mature in life and as you mature in Christ. One of my old youth pastors used to say, "New levels, new devils" and scripturally you can say we go from faith to faith (Romans 1:17). Which all means, you passed that level of challenge, that level of faith, but now it is time to experience something else that requires a greater level of faith. Unfortunately, but what is not growing, is dying.

All Is Possible With FAITH

Luke 1:37 "For with God, nothing shall be impossible"

My Faith and confidence in that I did not have to tolerate my peace being stolen was because of the word of God. The scriptures are my evidence. God cannot lie. Your best bet against any challenge you face in life is to pray or fight back using the sword of the Spirit which is the Word of God. His word cannot return to Him void, meaning it must produce what He said it will produce.

I want to instill in your head and heart that it is NOT the will of God for us to be sick. It is NOT the will of God for us to be worried. It is NOT the will of God for us to be afraid of the things in this world. It is NOT the will of God for us to be tormented. Those things are from the adversary.

Meditating on the Word must become our lifestyle. We must eat, sleep, and drink the Word. I pray you choose to take authority over your life today and stop tolerating what God said you do not have to tolerate. So many of us are living limited lives, suffering because we do not know what God says. His word says my people perish for the lack of knowledge (Hosea 4:6). Meaning people have died of sicknesses and been institutionalized simply because they did not know what God said about healing and having His mind and peace. It is a lie to say that someone having a sickness or lack of peace is glorifying God. How does something that God sent Jesus to the Cross for glorifies Him? If that's the case, Jesus died for nothing.

God says without Faith, we cannot please Him (Hebrews 11:6). There must be no doubt in the fact you can overcome and defeat anxiety. It is His will to heal you from all sickness and disease. It is His will that you have His mind and His peace. How does one build faith? By reading and hearing the word of God. Daily.

NOW, FAITH IS ..... meaning Faith is always present tense. The faith you had yesterday is not the faith you have today.

Meditate Until Breakthrough

Use these scriptures, make them personal as shown, and meditate on them for the rest of your life. Get them down in your spirit, in your heart, and in your mind. Believe this Truth and you will be set free. (John 8:32)

1. <u>Philippians 4:13</u> "I can do all things through Christ who strengthens me."

2. <u>Isaiah 53:5</u> "But He was pierced for our transgressions, He was crushed for our iniquities; the punishment which brought us peace was on Him, and by His stripes we are healed and made whole."
   - *Declare: Heavenly Father in Jesus name, I decree that I am healed and whole by the stripes Jesus took for me. Amen*

3. <u>Philippians 4:7</u> "and the peace of God which transcends all understanding, will guard your hearts and your minds in Christ Jesus."
   - *Declare: Heavenly Father in Jesus name, I decree I have the peace of God. Amen*

4. <u>1 Corinthians 2:16</u> "……but we have the mind of Christ."

   ➢ *Declare: Heavenly Father in Jesus name, I decree I have the mind of Christ. Amen*

5. <u>Psalms 34:4-5</u> "I sought the Lord, and He answered me and delivered me from all my fears….."

6. <u>Psalms 23:4</u> "Even though I walk through the valley of the shadow of death, I will fear no evil, for You are with me; Your rod and Your staff, they comfort me."

7. <u>Psalms 27:1</u> "The Lord is my light and my salvation; whom shall I fear? The Lord is the stronghold of my life; of whom shall I be afraid?"

8. <u>Psalms 46:1</u> "God is our refuge and strength, a very present help in times of trouble."

9. <u>Isaiah 41:13</u> "For I, the Lord Your God, hold your right hand; it is I who say to you, "Fear not, I am THE ONE, who helps you."

10.   <u>Luke 14:27</u> "Peace I leave with you; my peace I give to you. Not as the world gives do I give to you. Let not your hearts be troubled, neither let them be afraid."

11.   <u>Psalms 91:2-6</u> "I will say of the LORD, "He is my refuge and my fortress; My God, in Him I will trust." Surely He shall deliver you from the snare of the fowler And from the perilous pestilence. He shall cover you with His feathers, And under His wings you shall take refuge; His truth shall be your shield and buckler. You shall not be afraid of the terror by night, Nor of the arrow that flies by day, Nor of the pestilence that walks in darkness, Nor of the destruction that lays waste at noonday."

> *Decree: Heavenly Father in Jesus Name, I decree that no evil shall befall me. Amen*

12.   <u>Deuteronomy 3:22</u> "You shall not fear them, for it is the Lord your God who fights for you."

13.   <u>Joshua 8:1</u> "And the Lord said to Joshua, "Do not fear and do not be dismayed."

14.   <u>Psalms 115:11</u> "You who fear the Lord, trust in the Lord! He is their help and their shield."

15.   <u>Isaiah 41:10</u> "Fear not, for I am with you; be not dismayed, for I am Your God; I will strengthen you, I will help you, I will uphold you with My Righteous right hand."

16.   <u>Exodus 15:26</u> "........I am the Lord who heals you."

17.   <u>Psalms 103:2-3</u> "Bless the Lord o my soul and forget not all His benefits; Who

forgives all your iniquities, Who heals all your diseases."

18.	Psalms 107:20 "He sent His word and healed them and delivered them from their destructions."

19.	Hebrews 6:18 "It is impossible for God to lie."

20.	Numbers 23:19 "God is not a man, that he should lie; neither the son of man, that he should repent: has He said and not done it? Or has he spoken, and will He not make it good?"

21.	John 16:33 "I have said these things to you, that in Me you have peace. In the world you will have tribulation. But take heart; I have overcome the world."

22.   Psalms 4:8 "In peace I will both lie down and sleep; for You alone, O Lord, make me dwell in safety."

23.   Daniel 10:19 "Fear not, peace be with you; be strong and of good courage."

24.   John 14:27 "Peace I leave with you; My Peace I give to you. Not as the world gives do I give to you. Let not your hearts be troubled, neither let them be afraid."

25.   Romans 5:1 "Therefore since we have been justified by faith, we have peace with God through our Lord Jesus Christ."

26.   Philippians 4:6 "Do Not be anxious about anything, but in every situation, by prayer and petition, with thanksgiving, present your requests to God."

27.   2 Timothy 1:7 "For God has not given us a spirit of fear, but gives us a spirit of power, love, and a sound mind."

28.   Hebrews 11:1 "Now faith is confidence in what we hope for and assurance about what we do not see."

These were just a few scriptures that I carried with me, however, there are plenty more scriptures in the Bible about peace, healing, faith, and not fearing. Do your due diligence and search the scriptures for yourself and write down more that resonates with whatever season of your life that you are in. My prayer in Jesus' name is that you will trust God, develop your relationship with Him through prayer, and mature in Christ and become Sons.

May the God of Hope fill you with all joy and peace in believing, so that by the power of the Holy Spirit, you may abound in hope."
(Romans 15:13)

Copyright

All scripture quotations, unless otherwise indicated, are taken from the Holy Bible.

All definitions have been rightly credited within the text.

Acknowledgments

I just want to give honor and praise to God, my Father, who loves me and only wants the best for me. My protector, healer, comforter, and provider. I thank You God for Your never-failing word that continues to keep me grounded and sane in this insane world. I thank You that there is NO ONE like You.
 In Jesus name, Amen